NATIONAL GEOGRAPHIC

Melting Away

PATHFINDER EDITION

By Glen Phelan

CONTENTS

Melting A

Temperatures are rising worldwide, which is causing weather to change. It is also affecting wildlife.

By Glen Phelan

jay

Glacier National Park in Montana is a place of beauty, with it's towering cliffs, jagged ridges, and deep valleys. All these features were made by ice.

That's right: Ice carved the rocks. Of course, small pieces of ice could not do all that, but giant ice sheets could and did. Ice still covers some parts of the park.

Ice at Work

Ice sheets form when more snow falls in winter than can melt in summer. Year after year, the snow piles up high, and huge mounds cover the land, while the bottom layers of snow slowly turn into ice.

When the ice grows heavy enough, it starts to move downhill, which is when a sheet of ice becomes a **glacier**. People often describe glaciers as "rivers of ice." Some glaciers were once more than a mile thick, and only the highest mountains poked through the giant ice sheets.

This has been happening at Glacier National Park for millions of years. Glaciers have slowly moved across the land, changing the landscape. They plowed away the soil, ground down mountains, and carved out valleys.

Glaciers don't last forever, though, because if the weather heats up, they melt. That happened at Glacier National Park about ten thousand years ago, and it is happening again today.

Warmer Waters. *Melting snow and ice formed this lake in Glacier National Park.*

© DAVID MUENCH, CORBIS

I'm Melting

Today, 26 glaciers cover parts of the park, and those glaciers are still changing the land.

The park's glaciers, however, are in danger of melting away. Take Grinnell Glacier, for instance. It's the most famous one in the park.

In 1910, Grinnell Glacier covered almost 440 **acres**. But by 1931, it had shrunk to 290 acres, and in 1998, only 180 acres remained. Water from the glacier has formed a new lake in the park.

At this rate, the once mighty Grinnell Glacier could soon vanish completely, and so could the park's 25 other glaciers.

Turning Up the Heat

Why is Grinnell Glacier wasting away? It's simple: The park is getting warmer. Since 1910, the average summer temperature there has risen more than three degrees Fahrenheit (F).

The park isn't the only place that's warming up. Most scientists agree that the rest of Earth is slowly warming up, too, and that rising surface temperature is called **global warming**.

Since 1850, Earth has warmed by about one degree F, and some places, such as Glacier National Park, have warmed up more. Some have warmed up less.

Worldwide Warming

One degree may seem small, but it is causing big changes worldwide. In the Antarctic and Arctic, sea ice is melting. The meltdown forms clouds that can make more snowfall than usual, and more snow can harm wildlife.

Penguins in Antarctica are having a hard time finding a place to lay eggs. They normally lay eggs on dry ground in the spring, but more snow is falling today. So the penguins have to lay their eggs in the snow, and when it melts, the snow water rots many of the eggs. That's causing the number of penguins to drop.

Trouble in the Tropics

Earth's warmer areas are also affected. Tiny animals called **coral polyps** build huge reefs in warm ocean water. Reefs come in many different colors. Fish dart around the reefs and lots of other creatures call coral reefs home, but many coral reefs are in trouble.

Because of global warming, ocean water is heating up, and if the water near a reef gets too warm, the polyps die and the once colorful reef turns white. When a reef dies, fish and other creatures have to find new homes, or they die, too.

Snack Food. *An American hare munches on springtime grass in a meadow in Glacier National Park.*

What's Going On?

No one is sure what is causing the worldwide warm-up. Most scientists blame some gases in Earth's atmosphere. They point to one gas in particular—carbon dioxide.

That gas keeps our planet warm by trapping heat from the sun. If there isn't enough of the gas, temperatures go down, but if too much carbon dioxide builds up, temperatures rise.

Many things make carbon dioxide. For example, erupting volcanoes make it. Cars, trucks, factories, and power plants also make it. All these things combined may be causing the gas to build up in Earth's atmosphere.

Some scientists blame the sun, —they say its temperature can change, and right now, it is warming up. This also happened 1,000 to 500 years ago, but then the sun cooled. Now the sun and Earth are warming again.

The Meltdown

If the warming continues, glaciers in Glacier National Park will continue to melt. Of course, the park will still be there, but the glaciers will be gone.

The melting glaciers could push wildlife out of the area. Grizzly bears are one example. They often move into the park's meadows to eat berries and other favorite snack foods.

Huge **avalanches** make the meadows. An avalanche happens when lots of snow suddenly crashes down a mountainside. The crashing snow tears down trees, giving berry bushes a place to grow. Without avalanches, there will be fewer berries and that means fewer bears. And bears are just one of the many animals affected by global warming.

The warming trend could affect many plants and animals because it is happening very fast. Some plants and animals might have to find new homes, and others might die out, or become **extinct.** To survive, they will all have to find ways to beat the heat.

? *How is global warming changing Earth? Who is affected by global warming?*

Wordwise

acre: measurement of land

avalanche: lots of snow suddenly crashing down a mountain

coral polyp: tiny animal that builds coral reefs

extinct: completely gone

glacier: large river of ice

global warming: worldwide rise in temperature

DAVID A. HARVEY/NATIONAL GEOGRAPHIC/GETTY IMAGES

Arctic Sea Ice Coverage

Rising temperatures have affected the huge sheets of ice surrounding the North Pole. These images show how.

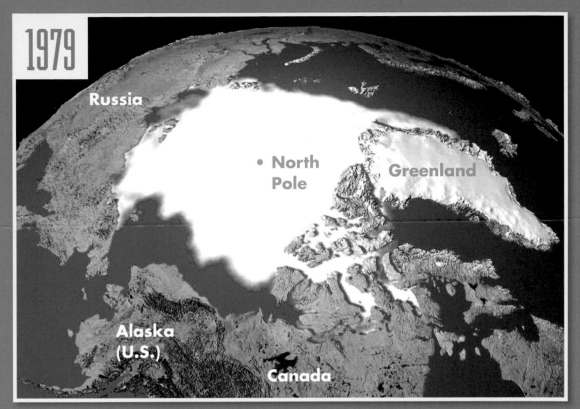

1979

Russia

• North Pole

Greenland

Alaska (U.S.)

Canada

In 1979, ice covered much of the Arctic throughout the year.

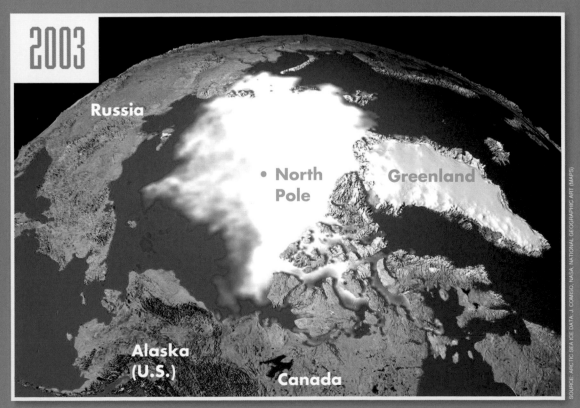

2003

Russia

• North Pole

Greenland

Alaska (U.S.)

Canada

By 2003, large amounts of ice had melted. Where there was once solid ice, there is now ocean water, and many scientists say the ice in the area will continue to melt.

SOURCE: ARCTIC SEA ICE DATA-J. COMISO, NASA; NATIONAL GEOGRAPHIC ART (MAPS)

Global Warnings

Most scientists say Earth is heating up. That means changes all over the world. This map shows you a bit of what's happening.

★ **Utah** Western states have been very dry. As a result, Lake Powell has much less water than usual.

★ **Virgin Islands** Warmer weather is causing problems for sea turtles. Many more females are hatching than males, and scientists don't know how that will affect sea turtle populations.

NORTH AMERICA

★ Hudson Bay

★ Utah

NORTH ATLANTIC OCEAN

★ Virgin Islands

SOUTH AMERICA

SOUTH PACIFIC OCEAN

SOUTH ATLANTIC OCEAN

★ Argentina

Antarctic Peninsula ★

★ **Argentina** Rising temperatures and water shortages have sparked massive wildfires in recent years.

★ **Hudson Bay** Winter ice melts two to three weeks earlier than before, and that makes it harder for polar bears to find food.

★ **Bangladesh** In 1998, rain flooded more than half the country. In 2003, floods drove 2.5 million people from their homes.

RCTIC OCEAN

EUROPE

ASIA

RICA

★Bangladesh

NORTH PACIFIC OCEAN

★Kenya and Tanzania

INDIAN OCEAN

★Great Barrier Reef

AUSTRALIA

NTARCTICA

NG MAPS

★ **Kenya and Tanzania** Malaria, a deadly disease which is carried by mosquitoes, is spreading. Mosquitoes thrive in warmer weather.

★ **Antarctic Peninsula** Winter temperatures are nine degrees higher now than they were in 1950. Sea ice has shrunk by a fifth. These changes make it much tougher for Adelie penguins to survive, and bird populations are sinking.

★ **Great Barrier Reef** Ocean water is slowly growing warmer, and the heat is hurting and even killing big pieces of the world's largest coral reef.

9

Warming Up

Earth is getting warmer, and many scientists think it's our fault. Their studies show that humans might be at least partly to blame, but we might also be part of the solution.

How do scientists study global warming? They look to the sky because the atmosphere gives clues about why Earth is heating up. The atmosphere is a blanket of gases around Earth, and some of these gases, such as carbon dioxide, trap heat.

Driving Up Temperatures

Most people depend on oil, coal, and natural gas. These fuels help run cars, heat homes, and power factories, but they also give off carbon dioxide. Carbon dioxide heats the atmosphere and makes Earth warmer.

Over time, cars and factories have changed the atmosphere. Today, the air has about 30 percent more carbon dioxide than in the days before cars and factories. Other heat-trapping gases have also skyrocketed.

Chopping Down Trees

Each year, people cut down a lot of trees for paper and wood. This is a problem because forests actually help lower carbon dioxide levels, as trees use carbon dioxide to make their own food.

When people cut down forests, more carbon dioxide hangs around in the atmosphere, which drives temperatures even higher.

Trashing the Land

People also produce a lot of trash. Most of it gets dumped into landfills. These are areas filled with trash and then covered with dirt.

As trash sits in landfills, it makes methane gas. The methane rises into the air and traps heat. More trash means more methane, and more methane means a warmer Earth.

The message, scientists say, is clear. People need to change their ways—beginning now, not next year. The future of Earth is at stake.

Ways to Slow the Warming

Reduce, reuse, recycle. You can help slow the warming by recycling newspapers, cardboard, glass, and metal. More recycling means that less energy is used to make products.

Spend less time in the car. Your family can give the car a day off. Instead of driving, you can take a bus, ride a bike, or share a ride with someone else.

Buy products that use less energy. For example, some lightbulbs use less electricity than others, and some last longer than others, too. Buy only energy-saving products.

Plant trees. Trees use carbon dioxide to make their own food, so planting more trees could help slow global warming. More trees could lead to less carbon dioxide in the air.

Teach others. Share what you know about global warming, and tell other people about ways to save energy and reduce trash. Together you can make an even bigger difference.

CHRISTIAN NOVAL, SHUTTERSTOCK.COM (PAGE 10); P.JIM JURICA, SHUTTERSTOCK.COM (RECYCLE); JASON STITT, SHUTTERSTOCK.COM (CAR); PETER HANSEN, SHUTTERSTOCK.COM (BULB); SUZANNE TUCKER, SHUTTERSTOCK.COM (SEEDLING); SUZANNE TUCKER, SHUTTERSTOCK.COM (TEACH)

Global Warming

Answer the questions to see what you've learned about this hot topic.

1 What causes ice sheets to form?

2 How can glaciers change land?

3 What is causing Grinnell Glacier to waste away?

4 Does global warming affect only cold, icy places? Explain.

5 How does carbon dioxide relate to global warming?

© DIGITAL VISION